LEARN
MOUNTAIN BIKING
IN A WEEKEND

LEARN
MOUNTAIN BIKING
IN A WEEKEND

ANDY BULL

Photography by Philip Gatward

DORLING KINDERSLEY
London • New York • Stuttgart • Moscow

A DORLING KINDERSLEY BOOK

Designer Emma Boys
Editor Deborah Opoczynska
Series Art Editor Amanda Lunn
Series Editor Jo Weeks
Managing Editor Sean Moore
Managing Art Editor Tina Vaughan
Production Controller Deborah Wehner/Helen Creeke

First published in Great Britain in 1992
by Dorling Kindersley Limited,
9 Henrietta Street, London WC2E 8PS
First paperback edition published in 1996
Copyright © 1992 Dorling Kindersley Limited, London
Text copyright © 1992 Andy Bull
Reprinted 1994

Visit us on the World Wide Web at
http://www.dk.com

A CIP catalogue record for this book
is available from the British Library

ISBN 0-86318-936-9
ISBN 0-7513-0428-x Pbk

Computer page make-up by
Book Production Services
Reproduced by Colourscan, Singapore
Printed and bound in Singapore by
KHL Printing Co Pte Ltd.

CONTENTS

INTRODUCTION

I WILL NEVER FORGET my first mountain biking weekend. I was in the English Lake District and hadn't been on a bike in years. I was totally unfit. We set off after breakfast to tackle the foothills of Skiddaw, which is 931m (3053ft) high. It would be simple, I was told, a chance for me to get the feel of the bike. Within ten minutes I was exhausted. The 21 gears totally confused me, my legs were quivering, my lungs felt tight, and my stomach was in turmoil.

Don't let this put you off, just don't start the way I did! It is perfectly possible to become a competent mountain biker in a weekend, but you need to prepare carefully if the time is not to be wasted. Having ridden everywhere that I could in England – all over the mountains of the Lake District, the moors of the West Country, the downs in the South – I decided I wanted to go to where the sport began, in the mountains of Marin County, northern California. Riding high above the Pacific was a magical experience. I went further afield, to the Badlands of South Dakota and the ski resorts of Colorado. The further afield I went, the more I came to realize how many fantastic places there are to mountain bike, around the world. There is a lifetime's cycling out there, thousands of adventures to have, hundreds of friends to be made. Mountain biking is quite simply one of the best ways to have fun on two wheels. Despite my problematic introduction to the sport, I was hooked, and I have never met anybody who, having been out on a mountain bike once, does not go out time and time again. With the skills in this book mastered, you can go on to do anything from simply enjoying the outdoors to having great adventures. You might take up the sport competitively, you might become a stunt rider. Anything can happen!

Andy Bull

ANDY BULL

PREPARING FOR THE WEEKEND

An introduction to the essential preliminaries

SHOOTING OFF on your mountain bike without considering the preliminaries is foolhardy. It is well worth delaying the adventure for a few weeks while you prepare properly. If you do not have the correct clothing you may get cold and wet, or hot and bothered. Either way, your enjoyment will be lessened and you could also be opening yourself up to danger. Venture out onto an exposed mountain in cold and wet weather without warm, waterproof clothing and you could very quickly fall victim to hypothermia. Take care in hot weather too, as vigorous or prolonged cycling on a hot day can cause overheating which can also be very serious.

DRESS SENSE
No matter what the weather conditions are when you set off, always wear a number of layers, so you can peel them off as you warm up and slip them on when you get cold (p.13).

CYCLE FIT
The best form of physical preparation for your cycling weekend, is cycling itself, even if it is on the spot (p.31).

TYRE PRESSURE

This is important. Too hard and you bounce all over the place, too soft and you risk punctures (p.18).

The rigours of off-road riding place particular strains on the body. The best way to prepare for them is to get used to cycling before the weekend. The machine you are riding also needs to be prepared. If your bike has not been thoroughly checked over since it was last ridden, it may let you down or even cause an accident. Learn how to give your bike a proper examination and you will minimize the possibility of anything going wrong. Always take the correct tools with you so that you can cope with any of the minor breakdowns that may occur. You need to be able to carry out running repairs and make the adjustments to the bike that rough riding can make necessary. Study the opening pages of this book and you will be!

LIMBER UP

Always carry out some loosening up exercises before setting out on a ride. This will warm your muscles and get you ready for the rigours to come (p.30).

A GOOD PLACE TO LEARN

For your first off-road ride, an area of gently sloping grassland with one or two obstacles to practice on is ideal. You do not want to tackle terrain so extreme that you cannot cope, you won't learn anything and are more likely to have an accident instead (pp.28-29).

TOOL KIT

A few basic tools will enable you to cope quickly with minor mishaps like removing a split link from a chain (p.20).

WHAT BIKE?

How to recognize a good quality, suitable bike

TRADITIONALLY, BIKES HAVE BEEN seen as very cheap and functional modes of transport. Mountain bikes are different. They offer far more in terms of higher quality and superior performance, and so naturally cost more. Even if you are not sure you will take to the sport, and are worried about wasting your money, do not make the mistake of buying the cheapest mountain bike you can find. It will not boast the qualities of a true mountain bike. Instead, rent, borrow, or buy a good quality second-hand machine.

COST OF QUALITY

Beware of cheap cycles masquerading as mountain bikes. A bike that costs far less than the standard price, will probably not be tough enough. Tell the shop assistant you want a basic bike for sustained off-road use. Manufacturers are competing hard for your custom, so shop around.

• FRAME
A good frame is essential for a strong but light bike. Examine the joints of the frame for cracks in the welding.

• HANDLEBARS
The handlebars are straight and wide for precision control of the bike. Make sure the grips are firm and comfortable.

• SADDLE
A poor saddle leads to discomfort and injury. It should be firm, supportive, and neither too wide nor too narrow.

GEARS
A 21-speed gearing system of a reliable make does not have to cost the earth. The Japanese are leaders in the field, yet are not the most expensive.

• TREAD
Tyres with a knobbly tread will maximize traction.

• TOE CLIPS
Toe clips are important for off-road riding.

FRAME SIZE

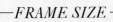

The longer saddle stem compensates for the smaller frame

Can you reach the handlebars easily?

It is vital to get a bike that is the right size. Mountain bike frames are usually 7–10cm (3–4in) smaller than standard sports bikes, to reduce weight and make the bike easier to manoeuvre. As a rough guide to the correct frame size for you, take your inside leg measurement and deduct 33–38cm (13–15in) from that figure. The frame measurement is made along the **seat tube**, from the centre of the **bottom bracket** to the centre of the **top tube**. When you stand astride the frame, there should be at least 2–5cm (1–2in) of clearance between the top tube and your crotch. When sitting in the saddle, you should be able to reach the handlebars comfortably.

BUYING A SECOND-HAND BIKE

Buying a second-hand bike can save you a lot of money, but take great care to ensure you don't buy an unreliable or even dangerous machine. The one shown below has bent and broken **spokes**, and the frame seems to have undergone a poor repair. If possible, take a knowledgeable friend along, and always insist on a test ride.

• BRAKES & GEARS
Do a test ride to ensure the brakes and gears work.

• TREAD
Uneven tyre wear can indicate that the bike has endured a great deal of punishment.

• FRAME
Check the frame joints for cracks in the welds.

• FORKS
Ensure the forks are not bent out of line.

• WHEELS
Look for buckles by lifting the bike and spinning the wheels.

• CRANK
Pull and push the end of the **crank** to reveal any play in the **bottom bracket**.

CLOTHING & EQUIPMENT

Specialized clothing & equipment for safety & comfort

MOUNTAIN BIKING can take you away from civilization, to where the terrain may be inhospitable and the weather severe. Having the right clothing and equipment minimizes your chances of getting into trouble, and maximizes your chances of solving any problems that do arise. If you cannot keep warm and dry, or are unable to fix a simple breakdown, your enjoyment, and cycling are likely to be curtailed.

TOOL KIT

Most repairs are quick and easy to make. Just a few basic tools can get you out of all sorts of problems. Tools are best carried in a backpack rather than in **panniers** or other large bags, which would weigh a bike down.

COOL TOOL

The essential tools – **Allen keys** (a), cone spanner (b), **crank** tool (c), chain breaker (b/d), headset spanner (e), and **bottom bracket** tool (f), are all combined in this Cool Tool.

• PUMP
A pump is vital, and not just in the case of punctures. The punishment that tyres get on rough ground means they can become deflated.

• TYRE LEVERS
A set of three tyre levers will enable you to remove a tyre without causing damage to it, or the inner tube.

• D-LOCK
Use a D-Lock to anchor the bike's frame, and possibly also the rear wheel, to an immovable object.

• PUNCTURE REPAIR KIT
A puncture repair kit should include a number of different sized patches, a tube of rubber solution, sandpaper for the area around the hole, and chalk for dusting the repair so that it does not adhere to the inside of the tyre.

• 6-IN-1
These **Allen Keys** and screwdrivers form one of many combinations of essential tools.

• CHAIN TOOL
This chain breaker, for removing link rivets, enables you to fix a snapped chain easily.

• INNER TUBE
Carry a spare inner tube in case you get a puncture that is too severe to repair on the spot.

GETTING INTO GEAR

To ensure that you keep your body at a comfortable temperature at all times, wear layers you can remove or put on as the weather changes. The first layer should be cotton, the next, an insulating layer of wool or synthetic material and, finally, a protective layer that is waterproof. A helmet is vital for proper protection. Wear light shoes with a good grip.

— PRACTICAL POCKETS —

Inner tube •

• Map
• Cool Tool

Cycling tops, like the one above, with a series of elasticated-top pockets at the rear can be useful for carrying maps and small items of food, compact tools, and first aid gear. As with other items of cycling clothing, choose fabrics that are designed to draw sweat away from your body, keeping you dry and comfortable, however hard you exert yourself.

LIGHT TOP •
A light top will keep you cool in good weather but you will need more protection if the weather deteriorates.

JACKET •
A good quality protective jacket will keep the rain out and also allow sweat to evaporate.

• **HELMET**
The head is the most vulnerable part of a cyclist's body, so always wear a helmet.

SHORTS •
Cycle shorts are designed to fit snugly, and without seams at the crotch, to avoid chafing.

• **GLOVES**
Gloves keep your hands warm and also protect them from jarring.

• **LEGGINGS**
Leggings provide insulation but you will also need waterproof trousers.

• **SHOES**
Shoes should be light and waterproof, with prominent grips for wet and slippery ground.

KNOW YOUR MOUNTAIN BIKE

Identification of the component parts of a mountain bike

A CYNIC WOULD SAY that a flashy paint job, a set of knobbly tyres, and a high price tag are all that sets a mountain bike apart from a touring or a racing bike. In fact, mountain bikes are lightweight, durable machines, with low gears, powerful brakes, and sturdy frames carefully tailored to function well in the toughest terrain. That is not to say that a mountain bike does not have its uses on the road, its robustness has made it a firm favourite with city riders, who find that it stands up well to pothole-scarred city streets.

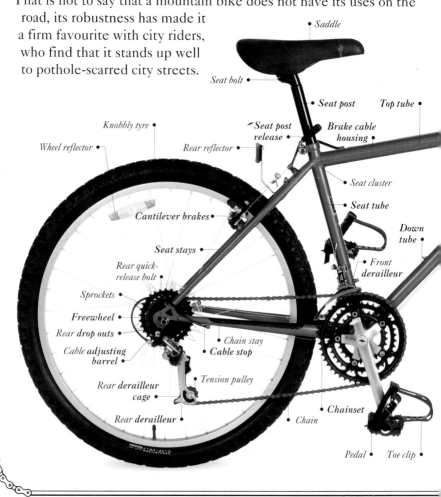

Saddle

Seat bolt

Seat post

Top tube

Knobbly tyre

Seat post release

Brake cable housing

Wheel reflector

Rear reflector

Seat cluster

Seat tube

Down tube

Cantilever brakes

Front derailleur

Seat stays

Rear quick-release bolt

Sprockets

Freewheel

Rear drop outs

Cable adjusting barrel

Chain stay

Cable stop

Rear derailleur cage

Tension pulley

Chainset

Rear derailleur

Chain

Pedal

Toe clip

RACING V. MOUNTAIN BIKES

The main differences between a racing bike, and a mountain bike stem from the fact that the former is built for speed, whereas the latter is built for strength and durability.

THE DIFFERENCES

The racing bike (right) is geared high for speed, while the mountain bike is geared low to cope with obstacles. The racer crouches low over the handlebars to reduce wind resistance, whereas the mountain biker sits back so that he can keep his weight off the front wheel which he frequently needs to yank up to clear objects and to get out of tight corners.

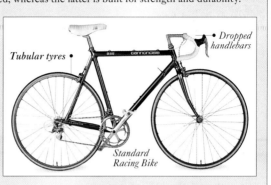

Tubular tyres •

• Dropped handlebars

Standard Racing Bike

SPECIAL QUALITIES

Several things set a mountain bike apart from a conventional bike. It has a much stronger frame, enabling it to stand up to rough country. The **bottom bracket** is higher, giving better ground clearance. Its knobbly tyres give it traction in wet, slippery, and unstable conditions. It has a sophisticated gearing system that enables a fit rider to power it up the steepest inclines and over the roughest terrain. It does not have mudguards because the **stays** would soon cause the wheels to be clogged with mud.

Handlebar • • Thumb shifter

Stem bolt • • Brake lever

Stem • • Grips

• Head tube

Cable stop • • Front reflector

• Fork crown

• Brake block

• Brake pivot bolt

• Fork blade

Front quick-release • • **Drop outs**
 • Wheel hub

• Nipple

• Spoke

Valve •

• Rim

Tread •

PREPARING THE BIKE

Making sure the bicycle is correctly adjusted

ADJUST THE BIKE to give you your optimum riding position, and ensure that the gears, brakes, and other moving parts are working correctly before you set off. This will help you avoid wasted effort and possible injury. It is important to have the saddle and handlebars at the correct height. A saddle that is too low can lead to knee injuries, one that is too high makes it difficult to apply maximum pressure on the pedals.

PRE-RIDE CHECKS

Before every ride, check that your brake blocks are not too far from the rim. If they are, turn the **adjuster barrels** anti-clockwise to bring them closer. If the brake blocks are worn down past their tread, replace them. Check that the quick-release on your saddle stem has not loosened. Put the front wheel between your knees and try to twist the handlebars to ensure that they have not worked loose. If you have your bike's owner's manual, consult it for specific advice about your particular machine.

HANDLEBAR HEIGHT
Using an **Allen key**, turn the stem expander bolt five times anti-clockwise, tap the bolt down, adjust the height, then tighten. You will also need to adjust the front brake cable.

ADJUSTING THE FRONT BRAKE
To make minor adjustments to the front brake cable length, turn the **adjuster barrel** on the brake lever. Turn anti-clockwise to tighten, clockwise to loosen.

SADDLE SURE
When you sit in the saddle, with your instep on one of the pedals, your leg should just be very slightly bent. Use the quick-release pin to adjust the saddle stem.

ALTERING THE FRONT BRAKE
For major alterations to the front brake, squeeze the brake arms together. This will release the **straddle cable**. Loosen the cable carrier and alter the cable length, then tighten it and reassemble.

BRAKE BLOCKS
The brake blocks should be between 1.6mm. and 3.2mm (1⁄16in and 1⁄8in) from the rim, and in line with it. Use an **Allen key** to loosen the blocks so that they can be aligned.

TYRE PRESSURE
The range of pressures for your tyres is printed on them, a typical range is 16–36kg (35–80lb) per 6.45cm^2 (1in^2).

PUMP IT UP

So long as the pump is the correct one for the type of valve on your tyre, pumping it up will be quick and easy. Reduce the chances of getting future punctures by regularly inflating your tyres to their correct pressure.

• *Presta Valve*

Schrader Valve •

VALVES
Loosen the barrel on the Presta valve to allow air to pass through. A car pump can be used on a Schrader valve which makes pumping up to high pressures much easier.

LUBRICATION

The working parts of a mountain bike, just like those of an engine, need to be kept clean and well oiled, in order to work smoothly. Water and mud quickly rob your bike of lubrication and once moving parts become dry they quickly start to wear, causing irreparable damage. Before and after each ride, clean and dry all the moving parts of the bike and then apply a spray lubricant, which will penetrate into the gearing mechanisms and bearings. In particular, spray a generous amount onto the **derailleurs**, chainwheels and gear sprockets, pedals, and **cranks**. Always take a small can of lubricant with you on your rides and use it if the bike gets thoroughly soaked.

QUICK-RELEASE BOLTS

Quick-release bolts are an advantage in that they enable the wheels to be removed swiftly and easily, either to make the bike easier to transport, for adjustment to wheel alignment, or for puncture repairs. Always remember to squeeze the brake arms and release the **straddle cable**, or the wheel will be held in place by the brake mechanism. After every trip, check that the quick-release bolts have not worked loose, as they can occasionally be knocked into the open position by rough riding.

FRONT WHEEL
To centre the front wheel, open the quick-release lever. This will allow you to adjust the wheel. Ensure that the axle is sitting snugly in the **drop outs** before closing the lever.

REAR WHEEL
If you have a quick-release bolt, proceed as above. If you have a bolt-on axle, use your spanners to loosen the nuts. Ensure that the wheel is centred and clears the brake blocks.

DERAILLEUR
The quick-release is undone as with the front wheel, but the **derailleur** obstructs the release of the wheel so has to be carefully pulled clear to allow it to move. As the derailleur is sprung-loaded, it will revert to its previous position once the wheel is removed.

TIGHTENING UP

If the pedals are loose, use an open ended spanner to turn the pedal axle clockwise. Adjust the toe clip straps, if fitted, so they are snug but not tight. With an **Allen key**, check the bolts attaching the chainwheels to the **crank**, are tight, the front **derailleur** is securely fastened to the **seat post**, and that the bolt attaching the rear derailleur to the **chain stay** is tight.

CRANKS
To check the **cranks** are tightly attached to the axle, remove the **bottom bracket dust caps** and turn the crank bolts clockwise.

RUNNING REPAIRS

How to cope with minor breakdowns

EVEN IF YOU CONSIDER yourself ignorant of all things mechanical, it is still a very good idea to learn at least enough about the workings of a bike to be able to repair minor problems like a puncture or a broken chain. If you can, then within a very short time you will be back on your bike. If you cannot, that may be the end of your day's cycling. What a waste! In fact, a bicycle is a very simple piece of machinery, and repairs are often very easy to make.

A BROKEN CHAIN

Exerting too much pressure on your chain can cause one of the links to break. To repair it, you really must have a chain breaker tool, so ensure there is one in the tool kit. Chains, especially those on a mountain bike, take a lot of punishment. If you have frequent problems, replace the chain.

1. THE BROKEN LINK
With the bike upside down, thread the chain onto the smallest chainwheel and the smallest rear sprocket. Wedge your knee against one of the pedals to stop the chainwheel rotating.

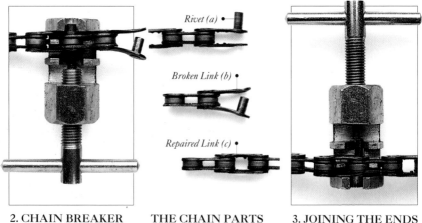

Rivet (a) •

Broken Link (b) •

Repaired Link (c) •

2. CHAIN BREAKER
Tighten the tool by turning the handle in a clockwise direction and push the rivet out until it is possible to remove the damaged link. Take care not to remove the rivet completely.

THE CHAIN PARTS
The rivet (a) has been pushed out until it is possible to remove the damaged link. The broken link (b) can now be removed and discarded. Use the chain breaker to join the two ends, (a) and (c).

3. JOINING THE ENDS
Hold the two ends together with the breaker in place and turn the handle clockwise. Push the rivet through the link until it is firmly in place. Make sure the newly joined link can move freely.

A PUNCTURE

To mend a puncture, place the bike upside down. Use your tyre levers to remove the tyre and pull the inner tube off the rim. The easiest way to find a puncture is to pump the tube up a little then submerge it in water and watch for bubbles coming from the hole, or you can run the tube past your ear and listen for a hiss. Remember to remove the object that caused the hole or, when you reassemble things, you will immediately get another puncture.

• REMOVE THE TYRE
Slip two tyre levers between the rim and the tyre, about 15cm (6in) apart, and lever a section of the tyre off the rim. Run a lever around the rest of the tyre to flip it all off.

1. PREPARE THE SURFACE
Use sandpaper to roughen the area of the inner tube around the hole, so that the adhesive can get a good grip.

2. APPLY THE SOLUTION
Smear rubber solution over an area slightly larger than the patch you are going to apply to the puncture.

3. APPLY THE PATCH
Once the solution is dry to the touch, peel away the protective film from the back of the patch. Press the patch firmly down onto the hole, using your thumbs.

4. HOLD IN PLACE
Smooth from the centre to the edges of the patch to expel air and press it in place for a minute or two.

REASSEMBLE •
Check the inner tube is not caught between the tyre and the rim.

REAR DERAILLEUR

Derailleur cables stretch with use and, as a result, it may no longer be possible to engage all of the gears. Most systems have a cable **adjusting barrel** and **travel limit adjuster bolts** to help ensure all the gears and the derailleur work smoothly.

TRAVEL LIMIT ADJUSTER

Low (a) and high (b) gear **travel limit adjuster bolts** ensure that the **derailleur** can move the chain to all of the gears, but will not let it move beyond them.

CABLE ADJUSTING BARREL

By turning the **cable adjusting barrel** anti-clockwise you may be able to take out the slack in the cable and enable all of the gears to be engaged. If, however, the cable is still slack, turn the barrel clockwise as far as you can, loosen the **cable clamp bolt** and pull the cable slack through. You can then tighten the bolt. Now adjust the barrel.

FRONT CABLE CLAMP BOLT

Turn the **adjusting barrel** to take up the slack cable. If this fails, then you will need to loosen the **cable clamp bolt** on the front **derailleur**, then pull the slack cable through. Using pliers will help. It should now be possible to engage all of the gears again.

FRONT DERAILLEUR

Like that of the rear **derailleur**, the cable on the front derailleur will need to be adjusted occasionally to take the cable slack out, similarly, bolts on the front derailleur can be altered to limit movement of the chain.

FRONT DERAILLEUR ADJUSTER

Low (a) and high (b) gear **adjuster bolts** mean you can set the front **derailleur cage** so that the chain will move between the chainwheels but not beyond them.

• ADJUSTER BARREL

Some systems have an **adjuster barrel** on the thumb shifter. If yours does, turn it anti-clockwise to take out slack in the cable. If it does not, adjustments will have to be made on the front **derailleur** itself.

A Buckled Wheel

A crash or prolonged hard riding may leave you with a wheel that is either egg-shaped or has a sideways buckle. Such distortions can be cured by adjusting the **spoke** tension. To assess the problem, spin the wheel and watch as it passes between the brake blocks. Check whether the rim moves from side to side or up and down.

• A Bad Buckle
With a very bad buckle, you may need to push the wheel roughly back into shape with your foot before making finer adjustments.

A SIDEWAYS WOBBLE
Where the wheel is buckled, use a **spoke** key to loosen the spokes leading to the hub **flange** that the wheel is bent towards. Tighten those leading to the other flange. Use half a turn at a time, repeat if necessary.

• FINAL CHECK
Remove the wheel and hold it before you, spin it and look carefully for any remaining kinks that need ironing out.

Correcting a Wheel

Loosen the **spokes** on the area of the wheel where the rim dips as you spin it, and tighten them at the point where the rim rises. Make half turns of the **spoke** key until the wheel spins true. Use the point where the wheel runs between the brake blocks as a guide.

SAFETY CODE

How to have a safe and trouble free weekend

BEING ABLE TO HANDLE your mountain bike well in difficult terrain is an essential skill, but you also need to be capable of navigating in unfamiliar territory. You must be able to read a map and to pinpoint your exact position. In poor weather, when fog may reduce visibility almost to zero, you need to be able to use a compass in conjunction with a map to find your way. All the dexterous cycling in the world will not help you if you don't have a clue where you are. In fact, such ignorance can be seriously dangerous.

THE ESSENTIALS

You may have no plans to be out after dark, but you should be prepared for delays, and, therefore, be ready to ride at night. Lights and reflectors are essential for safe riding in darkness or fog. They enable you to see and be seen. (See p.19 for essential clothing.)

BACKPACK •
You will need a good size backpack to carry rations, tools, and first aid equipment.

REFLECTOR •
Reflective clothing glows in the dark and so increases your chances of being seen.

REAR LIGHT •
A red, rear light ensures you can be seen.

• FRONT LIGHT
A front light is vital for finding your way, particularly in fog and over rough ground.

MAP READING

Being able to read a map is a must. An understanding of the symbols used, and the way the characteristics of the landscape are represented, will enable you to both pinpoint your position and locate your destination with ease. You will also be able to judge the severity of the terrain which you should take into account when estimating the time a particular trip is likely to take you.

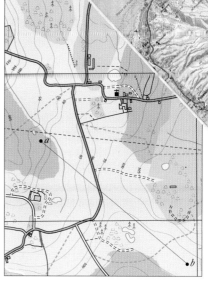

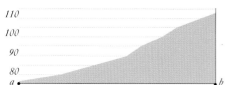

CONTOUR LINES
Contour lines illustrate how steep the terrain is. Learn to read them, and the map almost appears three dimensional.

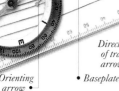

Aid lines •

Rotating compass
housing •

Direction
of travel
arrow •

• Baseplate

Orienting
arrow •

Magnetic
needle •

CHOOSING A MAP
The range of maps and charts now available is extensive. Choose a map that has easily identifiable colour codes, clear print, and is small enough to fit into your back pocket.

USING A COMPASS

Always carry a compass. You may never have to use it, but should you find yourself hidden in fog or totally lost, it can be your one sure way of getting out of trouble. The Silva compass is ideal for a mountain biker as it is light and simple to use yet does everything necessary.

KEEP ON THE PATH •
Check the reading to ensure you are sticking to your path.

OBTAIN A BEARING
To identify your position, lay the compass on the map with the baseplate parallel to the line on the map on which you wish to travel.

IDENTIFYING NORTH
Hold the compass in position on the map. Turn the dial until the "N" on it aligns with the direction in which the magnetic arrow is pointing.

MOVING OFF
The red orienting arrow points you in the direction you need to move off in. The letter aligned with this arrow indicates if it is N, E, S, or W.

MOUNTAIN CODE

Be a safe, environment-friendly off-road cyclist

MOUNTAIN BIKES can damage the environment. Knobbly tyres can chew up fragile terrain, skidding wheels can loosen rocks, speeding cyclists can frighten wildlife, as well as walkers and others who choose to enjoy the countryside in a different way. Worldwide, moves are now being made to restrict the freedom of mountain bikers. Each off-road cyclist is an ambassador for the sport. So, if we are to avoid being labelled "vandals" we must ride with care and consideration.

WILDLIFE
Some mountain bikers seem to think it is fun to scare livestock by racing past them. Show respect, consider the life of the countryside.

LEGAL PATHS
Only ride where you know you are allowed. A good map will identify bridleways, byways, and roads used as public paths. Use them!

MOUNTAIN CODE

Mountain codes may differ slightly from country to country, but the following are some of the most important rules. Use them to protect the countryside.

RULES
• Only ride where you know it is legal to do so, and where you can do no damage.
• Give way to pedestrians and horses.
• Do not damage crops. If a crop obscures a legal path, minimize damage.
• Take litter home with you. If others have left it, clear it up where possible.
• Do not light fires. Ensure cooking stoves cannot ignite undergrowth.
• Do not frighten animals.
• Use gates and stiles to cross fences where available, and close gates after you.
• When choosing your route, take care to avoid damaging plants and trees.

RISKY WEATHER

Do not try to learn to mountain bike when weather conditions are extreme. It will not be fun, and can be very dangerous. The weather can change fast on mountains. Clement conditions in the shelter of a valley can quickly be replaced by rain, high winds, low cloud, and low temperatures on an exposed mountainside. If you find that you are unable to keep warm and dry, are having trouble navigating, or find cycling conditions that you cannot cope with, abandon the trip.

FOG
Fog is a particular danger when you are out on a mountain. A sudden formation of mist or low clouds, can mean you get lost and may stumble into dangerous terrain.

SNOW
Riding over fresh, crisp snow can be truly exhilarating, but you should not attempt it unless you know the terrain well. Snow hides all sorts of hazards, from rocks to deep ravines. If you face deep, soft snow, give up, it is almost as hard to cope with as soft, dry sand.

EYES •
Keep a keen look out for mounds that may indicate hidden obstacles, as thick snow can conceal all kinds of hazards.

CYCLE CARE •
As with other difficult surfaces, aim to keep your wheels turning slowly. This minimizes the risk of spinning and loss of speed.

WHERE TO LEARN

Finding the right terrain for a beginner

WHEN YOU FIRST THOUGHT of going mountain biking you may have entertained visions of yourself conquering the rocky summit of a high, craggy mountain or plunging fearlessly from a peak to a valley, down an almost vertical drop. Well, you will get there in the end if you want to, but when you are learning you need terrain that will teach you, not beat you. The ideal is an area of open grassland with some inclines and a few basic obstacles that you can tackle, preferably where there is mud, water, loose and uneven surfaces, and some fallen trees.

BEGINNERS' TERRAIN
This is ideal beginners' country. Open spaces enable you to get used to handling the bike, while the everyday hazards such as rough ground and fallen trees in wooded areas, provide plenty of opportunity to practice your skills.

SAFE SLOPES

Riding on mountains is exciting, but unless you are an experienced rider, stick to the lower slopes where the inclines will not defeat a novice and the risks are not so great. Look for varied terrain that has mud as well as rocks.

PATH PRACTICE

With luck you will find one small area that enables you to practice several skills. This incline gives the rider practice using his 21 gears, going up and downhill, cornering at speed, coping with rough and loose ground, and, if he is unlucky, falling off without hurting himself. Nearby are large rocks and logs that he can practice hopping the bike over. However, wide paths like these cannot teach him everything. He also needs to tackle a narrow, winding track through woods to hone his handling skills.

REMOTE AREAS

For your first weekend away, you should not venture too far from civilization. If you must go somewhere remote, then go with friends, it will be both safer and more fun.

PATH NETWORK

If it isn't possible to get out into the open country, try to identify a network of paths on which you can legally cycle and which offers as many hazards as possible.

FIT TO RIDE

Before embarking on your weekend, get physically prepared

SOME PREPARATION BEFORE YOU set off on your weekend will ensure you enjoy yourself, and learn more than just the meaning of "saddle sore". Even if you regularly participate in other sports and consider yourself quite fit, mountain biking will make you aware of flabby muscles in places you didn't even know you had. It is important to build up your fitness, and to become accustomed to cycling, in the weeks before your weekend course. Follow the advice here and you will be ready for the challenge.

WARMING UP

A few warm up exercises before any vigorous sport will ensure your muscles are prepared for the rigours to come.

SPINE REFLEX
Touch your toes, keeping your knees as straight as is comfortable. Repeat.

THIGH STRETCH
Grip your foot and pull it up towards your buttocks. Repeat with the other leg.

• BENDS
Only make very slight bends.

• CALF
Feel the pull at the back of your calf.

SIDE STRETCH
With the left hand behind your head and the right hand on the right thigh, bend to the right several times. Change hands and repeat on the left side.

• POSTURE
Do not swing your hips and try not to lean forwards or backwards.

KNEE BEND
Place your hands on one thigh and flex the knee. Keep the other leg straight.

TURBO TRAINER •
A turbo trainer fits on
to the rear wheel of
your bike and allows
you to change gear
while still cycling.

GETTING FIT

The best preparation for cycling
is cycling itself, but there are other
useful and relevant exercises you
can do. Using a rowing machine
helps to strengthen the upper
back and arms. Training with
weights strengthens the
muscles, and sports
such as running
and swimming are
also beneficial.

RIDING
INDOORS
A stationary bike
enables you to keep
up your cycling even
when you are indoors.

INTERVAL TRAINING

This exercise is particularly suited
to off-road riding. Intersperse short
periods of riding the bike with short
bursts carrying it. Try it around a
football pitch. Cycle the length of the
pitch. Dismount. Pick up the bike,
placing it on your shoulder and
run to the far corner. Repeat. (See
p.50 for details of this method.)

• SHOULDER
Carry your bike
over your shoulder.

— GETTING STARTED —
Acclimatize yourself to cycling in the
two weeks or so before your weekend
course. Begin with gentle rides of
about a half hour, building up to more
rigorous outings of two to three hours.
These rides do not have to be off-road,
but if they are you will also get used
to riding on surfaces less reliable than
tarmac. Try to get in at least one half-
day ride before the weekend. If, in the
couple of days before the weekend,
you can cycle for half a day and tackle
steep hills without collapsing or feeling
exhausted, you have the basic level of
fitness and familiarity with cycling to
sail through the weekend.

RUNNING
Running, like
cycling, is good
for stamina and
strengthening
the legs.

BASIC FIRST AID

Coping with possible injuries and ailments

MOUNTAIN BIKING IS NOT inherently dangerous, but accidents can happen. The terrain you are riding through is likely to be demanding, and you will probably be at least a few miles from civilization. If something does go wrong, and a rider suffers an injury, or is having trouble coping with the riding or weather conditions, it is important to act fast. The following is a very brief introduction to the subject of first aid. It is a good idea to undertake some basic training.

ACHES & PAINS

If you suspect a limb may be broken, do not attempt to straighten it, or to move the patient until the fracture has been immobilised. Seek qualified help immediately. If the patient has cramp, massage the affected area and keep her warm. Cramp can be caused by a salt deficiency, so drinking a **saline solution** may help.

-FLAMING & FREEZING-

HEATSTROKE
Continuous, vigorous exercise in hot, dry weather can cause severe overheating. A person suffering from heatstroke can become confused, anxious and irrational, with a high pulse and respiratory rate. They should be cooled by removing their clothes, fanning, and placing wet clothing onto their head, body, and limbs.

HYPOTHERMIA
Prolonged exposure to cold weather can induce hypothermia. Symptoms include severe discomfort, shivering, and can lead to unconsciousness. Shelter the patient from rain, wind, and cold.

CUTS
Minor cuts should be cleaned and covered. With serious bleeding, apply direct pressure to the wound using a lint pad until the flow stops, then bandage.

HEAD INJURY

If a patient is unconscious or has a head injury, you should frequently check that their breathing is not obstructed. Remove false teeth and put the patient into the recovery position to prevent the tongue from falling back. Dress any wounds. Do not give the patient anything to drink.

LOWER LEG •
Position the patient on their side with the lower leg extended.

UPPER LEG •
Bend the other leg at the knee and bring it forward for balance.

LOWER ARM •
Tuck the lower arm in, close to the body.

• UPPER ARM
Bring the upper arm across the body.

BASIC FIRST AID KIT

You must take a basic first aid kit with you on your weekend away, even if you are only going to be just a mile or two from civilization. The sooner you can treat an ailment, the less likely it is to develop into something more serious. The kit should include plasters for cuts and blisters, lint or gauze for dressing wounds, bandages, antiseptic cream, **saline solution**, and a thermometer. It is important to get qualified medical help for an injury as quickly as possible. If someone in your party has basic first aid training, they should organize any immediate action.

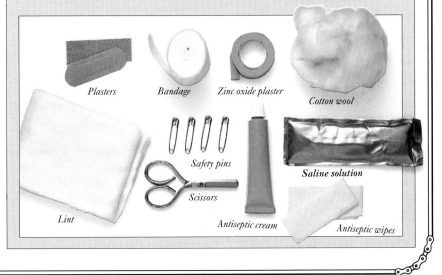

Plasters *Bandage* *Zinc oxide plaster* *Cotton wool*

Safety pins *Saline solution*

Scissors

Lint *Antiseptic cream* *Antiseptic wipes*

THE WEEKEND COURSE

At-a-glance timetable for the two-day mountain biking course

THE WEEKEND COURSE is divided into sixteen skills, and will take you two days of six hours each to complete. Riders with a particular aptitude for cycling may find that they can sail through the earlier skills in less than the time recommended. If you do get ahead of schedule, use the spare time for additional practice of the more challenging skills outlined on the second day of the course. The technical terms are highlighted in bold and explained in the glossary. Choose a weekend when reasonably good weather is forecast.

Shouldering your bike with ease (p.50)

Downhill riding (p.48)

DAY 1		Hours	Page
SKILL 1	Coping with 21 gears	$^1/_2$	36-39
SKILL 2	Pedalling technique	$^1/_2$	40-41
SKILL 3	Getting on & off	$^1/_2$	42-45
SKILL 4	Uphill riding	1	46-47
SKILL 5	Downhill riding	1	48-49
SKILL 6	Carrying your bike	$^1/_2$	50-51
SKILL 7	Cornering	$^1/_2$	52-53
SKILL 8	Riding across a camber	$^1/_2$	54-55
SKILL 9	Rocks & drops	1	56-57

KEY TO SYMBOLS

CLOCKS
The clock indicates how long to spend on the skill, and where it fits into your 6-hour day. The clock indicates how long to spend on the skill, and where it fits into your 6-hour day. The grey segment shows how many hours you have spent on other skills earlier in the day. The blue segment highlights the recommended time for the skill in question. If you find yourself taking far longer than the given time, there is no need to worry, just work at your own pace.

RATING SYSTEM •••••
Each skill is rated in terms of its relative difficulty on a scale of one to five. The bullets that appear against each skill show how much of a challenge it is likely to be. One bullet (•) denotes a skill that is relatively easy to acquire. As the number of bullets increases, so does the difficulty of the accompanying skill. The five bullet skills are the most challenging. Follow the individual steps of these skills carefully.

MICRO-BIKERS
The mini-sequence of micro-bikers at the start of each skill helps you to identify the individual steps of that particular skill. The blue micro-biker denotes the point within the manoeuvre that the accompanying photograph illustrates. The numerals above the figures, are the order of the sequence.

ARROWS
The arrows accompanying some of the photographs in the skills section are there to give an instant indication of how you should be using strength, weight, and balance during a manoeuvre. For instance, when riding uphill on loose ground, you must bear down in the saddle to maintain maximum traction (see p.47). The arrows confirm the point.

How to corner quickly and safely (p.52)

Hopping over logs and other obstacles (p.62)

1 GETTING TO KNOW 21 GEARS

Definition: *Mastering the gearing mechanism*

HAVING 21 GEARS to choose from may sound daunting, but in fact you rarely use more than two or three gears during a manoeuvre. The only times you are likely to be rapidly shifting through the whole range of gears is when conditions are changing fast.

OBJECTIVE: To use the full range of gears to the best advantage. *Rating* •

UNDER-BAR SHIFTERS

Push button gear shifters that are attached below the handlebar

• *Left hand*

Right hand •

FRONT DERAILLEUR CONTROLS
On the left, the top button takes you down to smaller chainwheels, the lower button takes you up to larger chainwheels.

REAR DERAILLEUR CONTROLS
On the right, each push of the top button or lever takes you down a gear. Each push of the bottom one brings you up one or more gears.

ON THE BIKE
Under-bar shifters are positioned near the brake and allow you to change gear and brake without having to relax your grip on the handlebars.

FRONT CONTROLS •
Give the lower front lever a delicate push to move from the large to middle chainwheels. A strong push is needed to move from the small to large chainwheels.

REAR CONTROLS •
The top button drops you down one cog at a time with ease, while the lower lever needs more pressure but enables you to sweep up several cogs at once.

THUMB SHIFTERS

Gear shifters that are attached above the handlebar

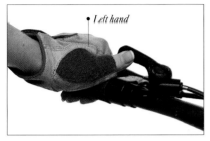

• *Left hand*

Right hand •

CHAINWHEELS – GOING UP

Push the left hand shifter away from you in an easy motion to move from the small to large chainwheels. The numbers beside the lever show you which chainwheel you are on.

REAR COGS – GOING UP

Push the lever away from you to move up the gears. The numbers that appear from one to seven beside the right hand shifter show you which gear you are in.

• *Left hand*

Right hand •

CHAINWHEELS – GOING DOWN

With your thumb behind the shifter, gently push it towards you to move from the large chainwheels to the smaller ones.

REAR COGS – GOING DOWN

Pull the shifter back towards you to move the chain to a lower gear. Shifting to larger cogs like this requires a much firmer pull.

ON THE BIKE

Serious riders tend to prefer above-bar shifters to under-bar shifters because they give an at-a-glance indication of which gear you are in. They are also easier to use when wearing gloves.

FRONT CONTROLS •

Moving from the largest to middle chainwheel takes a delicate touch, moving from the smallest to largest takes a strong push.

• REAR CONTROLS

Moving from the larger to smaller rear cogs requires a more delicate touch than the shift from smaller cogs to larger ones.

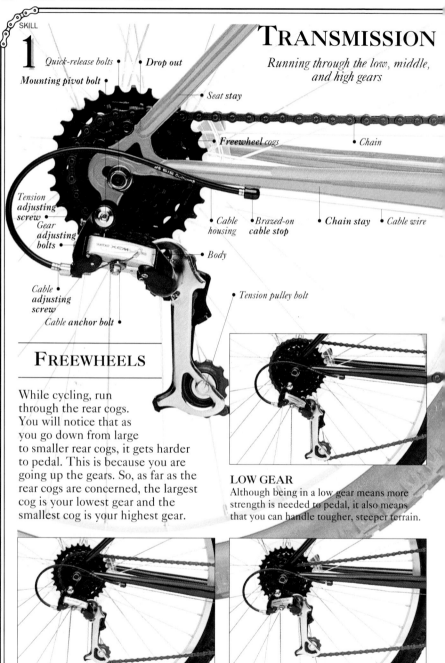

SKILL

1

Quick-release bolts •   • Drop out

Mounting pivot bolt •

• Seat stay

TRANSMISSION

Running through the low, middle, and high gears

• Freewheel *cogs*

• Chain

Tension
adjusting
screw •

Gear
adjusting
bolts •

• Cable
housing

• Brazed-on
cable stop

• Chain stay   • Cable wire

• Body

Cable •
adjusting
screw

Cable anchor bolt •

• Tension pulley bolt

FREEWHEELS

While cycling, run
through the rear cogs.
You will notice that as
you go down from large
to smaller rear cogs, it gets harder
to pedal. This is because you are
going up the gears. So, as far as the
rear cogs are concerned, the largest
cog is your lowest gear and the
smallest cog is your highest gear.

LOW GEAR
Although being in a low gear means more
strength is needed to pedal, it also means
that you can handle tougher, steeper terrain.

MID GEAR
Move from the large to smaller cogs as you
pick up speed. You will progressively be
moving up the gears as you accelerate.

HIGH GEAR
With the smallest rear cog engaged, you are
in the highest gear obtainable without
shifting to a larger front chainwheel.

• *Adjustable bolts*

• *Chain guide*

• *Chainring*

• *Chainring bolt*

• *Crank bolt*
dust cap

Cage bolt •

Spider •

CHAINWHEEL

You will notice that, again, as you go from the small to larger cogs, it gets harder to pedal. Therefore, as far as the front chainwheels are concerned, you are in the lowest gear when the chain is on the smallest chainwheel, and in the highest gear when the chain is on the largest chainwheel.

LOW GEAR
The smaller the chainwheel engaged, the lower the gear you are in. Use a low gear when starting or when the going is tough.

MID GEAR
Engage the middle chainwheel to tackle flat, but still difficult, terrain, shifting through the rear cogs as the going gets easier or harder.

HIGH GEAR
Move to the largest chainwheel to be in a high gear. If your chain is also on the smallest rear cog, you will be in your very highest gear.

2 PEDALLING TECHNIQUE

Definition: *Gaining maximum power from pedalling*

THINK OF YOUR LEGS and pedal **cranks** as two pistons in an engine. When one of the pistons starts pumping down, a surge of energy is relayed and you power forward. However, with only two thrusts of power available to you in each revolution of the pedals, there are periods when neither piston is in the powerful part of its stroke, and, as a result, there is less energy available to fuel the forward motion. The aim, in pedalling technique, is to smooth out these peaks and lift those troughs – to convert a jerky motion into a fluid rhythm.

OBJECTIVE: To obtain a smooth, fluid, efficient rhythm. *Rating* •

PEDALLING CYCLE

The three photographs to the right illustrate the pedalling cycle. In the first picture, the right foot is at the start of its pedal stroke. The left foot is in the lower, **dead spot** of the pedal stroke. While pressing down hard on the right pedal, bring the left pedal up through that dead spot. Point the toes of both feet down, and move them in a motion – as a horse does when pawing the ground – to push the pedal back and through the dead spot. In the second picture, the right leg is in the centre of its power stroke. Lift the left knee and flip your toes up against your toe clip. The third picture shows the right foot is in its dead spot and the left foot is at the start of its power stroke. Keep the heel of the left foot higher than the toes so that you can make a smooth transition between power strokes.

START OF POWER STROKE
The pedals are in the vertical position. The right foot is just passing the upper **dead spot**. Kick it forward to maintain momentum.

CYCLING TECHNIQUE
Cycling is not just about
strength and stamina, it is
also about technique. Even
when you reach the limits
of your physical ability,
you can still improve
your cycling by
concentrating on
developing your style.

• GEARS
The ideal pedalling
speed is 90rpm.
Move through the
gears as necessary
to maintain it.

• FEET
A smooth, pedalling rhythm
helps you to conserve energy.

CENTRE OF POWER STROKE
The pedals are now in the horizontal position.
Never dip your heel below the ball of your
foot, or you will reduce your efficiency.

END OF POWER STROKE
The right foot is now in its **dead spot**. Push
down with the ball, then the toes, of your
right foot. This calls up greater power.

GETTING ON & OFF

Definition: *Mounting, dismounting, and lifting smoothly*

THE IMPORTANCE OF GETTING on and off a bike correctly is often overlooked by cyclists. However, to be able to do so quickly and with the minimum of fuss will save time and frustration. This skill also teaches you how to dismount and lift your bike over your shoulder, in one fluid motion. A short while spent mastering these techniques will pay dividends later in improved efficiency, and give a far more professional appearance to your cycling.

OBJECTIVE: To increase speed, style and efficiency. *Rating •*

MOUNTING

To get on the bike and be ready to ride off in one fluid motion

――――― Step 1 ―――――
PREPARING TO MOUNT

Always get on the bike from the left side. This keeps you away from the oily gearing system and sharp cogs. Place both hands on the handlebars to help steady the bike.

• HANDS
Place both hands on the grips.

• BRAKES
On an incline, keep the brakes applied until you are ready to move off.

GEAR •
Ensure the gear you are in is low enough to get the pedals turning once you are on the bike.

LEG •
Your saddle is at
the right height
if you are able
to swing your
leg over it easily.

Step 2

FLUID MOTION

Holding the
bike steady,
swing your right leg over the
saddle. Press the toes of your
right leg onto the edge of the
pedal and slide your foot into
the toe clip. With practice, you
should be able to do this
in one smooth move.

RIGHT PEDAL •
Ensure the right pedal is near
the top of its power stroke.

• **HANDS**
Keep a light
touch on the
rear brake
until you
pedal.

Step 3

GETTING STARTED

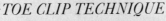

Once your right foot is in the
toe clip, press down on the
pedal, bringing your weight
over as you do so. Swiftly
put your left foot onto its
pedal. You can now slip into
a smooth pedalling motion.

TOE CLIP TECHNIQUE

CLIP UP
Press your toe on the side of the pedal
to bring the clip up to the horizontal.
This takes a little practice.

CLIP ON
With the pedal in the horizontal position,
slide your foot forward into the toe clip.
Keep your toes pointing down.

SKILL

3

DISMOUNTING

Getting off your bike with minimal loss of motion

———— Step 1 ————

PREPARING TO DISMOUNT

The object is to get off the bike and be running or walking with the machine in one fluid motion. Stop pedalling and begin to transfer all your weight onto your left foot.

• LEFT FOOT
With your left foot at the bottom of the pedal arc, start to bring your weight onto it and off your right foot.

RIGHT LEG •
Swing your right leg over the bike, maintaining your balance by shifting the bike to the right.

———— Steps 2 & 3 ————

LEAVING THE SADDLE

When coming out of the saddle, transfer all your weight onto your left leg. Swing your right leg back over the bike. Maintain the bike's balance by tilting it to the right, away from your body.

• LEFT LEG
Brace your left leg to take your full weight as you swing your right leg over.

SMOOTH DISMOUNT
For a smooth, quickly executed dismount, try to plan ahead. When you see that you are approaching an obstacle that is going to force you to dismount, coast up to it, get out of the saddle, and be balanced on one pedal as you reach it. In this way, you will be ready to get off the bike quickly and with the minimum of disruption to your progress.

Step 4

TOUCHING THE GROUND

Once your right foot is over the bike, bring it in front of your left foot. Just as the toe of your right foot touches the ground, transfer all of your body weight onto it, and remove the left toe from the toe clip.

ON THE GO
Dismounting while moving saves time.

• RIGHT FOOT
Bring your right foot over and in front of your left foot.

Steps 5 & 6

LIFTING THE BIKE

If the obstacle is minor, simply lift the bike over it and remount. If you need to carry the bike for a while, it is easiest to balance it on your shoulder.

LIFTING FOR A MOMENT
If you are merely lifting the bike for a moment, and the obstacle is not a high one, simply raise the cycle by grasping the **top tube** in your right hand and lift, steadying the bike with your left hand on the handlebar. However, shouldering the bike is the easiest way of carrying it for any distance, and leaves you with a free hand to steady your progress.

4 UPHILL RIDING

Definition: *The mountain biker's way of tackling inclines*

GOING UPHILL is where the difference between mountain biking and road cycling really becomes apparent. While the road cyclist will tackle a hill by getting out of the saddle and putting all his weight onto the pedals, the mountain biker must remain either in the seat, or with his bottom well back so that his weight is over the rear wheel. If he does not, he is likely to lose traction, the rear wheel will spin, and the hill will have defeated him. At first, the temptation to stand up on the pedals may be irresistible, but try to avoid it. You will quickly get used to remaining seated.

OBJECTIVE: To grasp one of the basics of off-road cycling. *Rating* ••

POSITION •
Keep your bottom in the saddle, or at least, hold your weight back.

GOING UP

Keep your behind back in the saddle to help centre your weight on the bike. Resist the instinct to pull up on the handlebars. If you do, the front wheel will lift, making it hard to keep your balance and to steer to your chosen course.

• **GEAR**
Get in a low enough gear to keep the pedals moving smoothly.

• **FRONT WHEEL**
Resist the desire to pull up the handlebars and front wheel, or you will lose balance and the ability to steer efficiently.

STEEP ASCENTS

POSITION
Keep your body weight centred on the bike to maintain traction of the rear wheel.

Adjust your body position to cope with the increasing steepness of the hill. Bend your elbows and bring your head down over the handlebars. In doing so, you will ensure that you keep good balance.

STEEP INCLINES
The steeper and rougher the incline, the more important it is to anticipate obstacles, plan a course, and steer it accurately.

• FEET
Keep up a fluid pedalling motion. The object is to keep moving, not to go fast.

THE DISTINCTION

Leaning over the handlebars removes weight from the rear wheel

With weight off the rear wheel, it may spin

Position of weight results in maximum pedalling power

THE WRONG WAY
This cycling position is disastrous for a mountain biker tackling a hill off-road. By standing on the pedals, she takes her weight off the rear wheel, which, if on a loose or slippery surface, will spin.

THE RIGHT WAY
A road cyclist on a good surface does not have to worry about losing traction, which means that his ideal riding position is one in which he can exert maximum pressure on the pedals.

5 DOWNHILL RIDING

DAY 1

Definition: *Maintaining balance while tackling a steep drop*

A MOUNTAIN BIKER will tackle descents that are far sharper than anything encountered on the road. Being able to navigate them successfully and safely, opens up one of the most enjoyable aspects of mountain biking. However, descents can be daunting to the novice. Balance is the major key to coping with them.

OBJECTIVE: To safely navigate a very steep slope. *Rating* •••

GOING DOWN

When going downhill, use the quick-release pin to drop the saddle down then slide your bottom well back onto it. This will help move the bike's centre of balance well to the rear and will also prevent you from toppling over the handlebars.

• BODY
Keep your body well back.

• HANDS
Brake with care. Use only the rear brake and avoid locking the rear wheel. If you skid, you will pick up speed again.

REAR WHEEL
On steep slopes, keep your weight well back in the saddle to ensure the rear wheel stays in contact with the ground.

TAKE DESCENTS SLOWLY

The arrows (right) show that the cyclist's weight distribution and position are not correct for a steep descent. To ride downhill safely, always follow these key rules:

• Take descents slowly. If you ride down a hill too quickly, just one small boulder could send you toppling over the handlebars.

• Do not lean forward, if you do, the rear wheel will lift, reducing traction and so increasing the likelihood of skidding.

• Keep upright. The more weight you have over the rear wheel, the greater the pressure you are able to apply on the brake without the wheel locking and going into a skid.

The rear wheel has a tendency to lift

STEEP DESCENTS

When the descent gets really steep, you may need to come right back off the saddle to maintain balance. The further back, and the lower you can get, the steeper the incline you can cope with.

A CAREFUL COURSE
On a very steep incline, pick out a smooth, safe path before descending, as just one rogue boulder under the rear wheel could tip you over the handlebars.

HANDS •
Do not use the front brake.

WEIGHT
When you go uphill, it is the front wheel that feels light, when you go downhill, it is the rear one.

• HEELS
Keep your heels pushed down to help maintain your position.

SKILL

6 CARRYING YOUR BIKE

Definition: *Shouldering the bike to navigate obstacles more efficiently*

ALTHOUGH THEY ARE "all-terrain" bikes, there are some surfaces that even mountain bikes cannot cope with, and no matter how great the challenge is to remain in the saddle, there will be times when you have to get off and carry the bike. The technique for carrying a bike, once mastered, will save you energy and frustration.

OBJECTIVE: To carry the bike readily and with ease. *Rating* •

———— Step 1 ————
PREPARING TO LIFT

Hold the bike with both hands and prepare to take its weight. Always stand to the left of it when lifting, so that you keep well away from the greasy chain and the sharp cogs of the chainwheels.

GOING UPHILL
If held correctly, a bike will be easy to carry, even up the steepest of slopes.

RIGHT HAND •
Cup your right hand under the **top tube**, just before the **seat post**, and grip.

LEFT HAND
Grip the handlebars just to the left of the handlebar stem.

Step 2
TAKING THE WEIGHT

Bending and lifting your right elbow, as if raising a dumbbell, bring the bike up to chest height with the saddle to the right of your face. At the same time, lift your left hand to raise the front wheel.

TROUBLE FREE
If you plan to be riding over tough terrain, avoid cluttering up your bike with bottle cages and pump brackets, which make the bike awkward to carry.

• **FRONT WHEEL**
The bike should be held at an angle, with the front wheel nearer the ground.

– AN AID TO CARRYING –

Frame cushion •

Bikes are usually cumbersome and awkward to carry. If you expect to have to carry the bike frequently or for periods of more than a few minutes at a time, use a frame cushion. These triangular bags fit in the angle between the **top tube** and **seat tube** and make carrying a bike more comfortable. They will also hold a compact tool kit. Some cyclists improvise by slipping a length of foam-rubber pipe insulation over both the top and seat tubes, securing it in place with insulating tape.

Steps 3 & 4
ONTO THE SHOULDER

Raising your right hand a little more, twist your right shoulder under the **top tube**, balancing the bike so that your left hand is merely steadying it.

ELBOW •
Keeping your elbow against the **down tube** helps hold the bike steady.

FRONT WHEEL •
Keep clean and safe by keeping the front wheel turned slightly away from your legs.

SKILL

7 CORNERING

DAY 1

Definition: How to take bends quickly and efficiently

A MOTOR RALLY DRIVER is far more adept at taking bends than the average motorist. To be a good mountain biker you need to be more adept at cornering than the average town cyclist. Being able to corner efficiently means you can keep up your momentum through bends, avoiding unnecessary braking and loss of speed.

OBJECTIVE: To take a corner as fast as possible. *Rating* • • •

────── Steps 1 & 2 ──────

THE APPROACH

EYES •
Keep your eye on the line of the bend.

Having approached the bend and slowed the bike to a safe speed, you then move your weight back and lean the bike as far into the bend as you feel is safe. Stick out the knee on the inside of the bend to aid balance.

PEDAL •
Keep the pedal on the inside of the bend at the top of its stroke. Do not try to pedal through a tight bend.

FOOTWORK
On a gentle curve, where there is no danger of the pedal hitting the ground, you can keep your feet in the horizontal position.

• GEARS
Before taking the corner, select the gear you will need to be in once the manoeuvre is completed.

Step 3
NEGOTIATING

If your balance is going, put down the foot on the inside of the curve. Skilled riders use a combination of rear brake and putting their foot down to bring the bike through a tight turn.

BODY POSITION •
Lean your body out of the bend and the bike into it.

• **KNEE**
Use the knee on the outside of the bend to aid balance.

• **HEEL**
If you feel you are losing your balance, dab the ground with the heel of your foot.

Step 4
LEAVING THE BEND

As you come out of the bend, shift your weight forward. Start pedalling as soon as you can. If you find you are not in the appropriate gear, select the correct one straight away, and regain your lost speed as quickly as possible.

PACE THE BEND

How swiftly you take a bend depends on your skill. Only go as fast as you feel is safe. Do not try to ride beyond your abilities. Instead, work to improve your confidence and skill. It is much better to lose a little speed on a bend than to take a tumble, especially in the early stages when it is easy to be discouraged. Practice tackling the same bend and you will find the speed at which you can take it will gradually increase.

• **GEARS**
As soon as you come out of the bend, move down to the correct gear.

BALANCE
Right the bike as you leave the curve, shifting your weight to the upright position.

8 RIDING ACROSS A CAMBER

Definition: *Taking a slope at an angle*

CYCLING OFF-ROAD is not all straight ups and downs. If you want to gain or lose height, you should ride across the slope diagonally. This is both safer and requires less effort than if you were to tackle the slope straight on. Resist the urge to ride downhill fast as this could result in either being thrown over the handlebars or being knocked out of your saddle by a stray boulder.

OBJECTIVE: To gain or lose height safely and smoothly. *Rating* ••

ACROSS A CAMBER

Riding across a **camber** is fairly straightforward except where the steepness of the slope makes traction hard to maintain. You can help prevent the wheels from slipping by moving your weight away from the slope.

KNEE •
To aid balance, swing out the knee nearest the slope.

HAND •
Avoid pressure on the grip that is away from the slope.

• PEDALLING
On a steep slope your pedal may hit the ground, making full pedal strokes impossible. Try to proceed with quarter turns of the pedals.

STEEP INCLINES
On a particularly steep incline it may be necessary to lean the bike well into the slope, bringing the saddle against the knee.

UPHILL

Tackle the uphill slope at a shallow
angle. Doing so maximizes traction
and lessens the danger of your pedal
hitting the ground. The aim is to
keep cycling, not to take the slope
at the sharpest, and toughest angle
possible which would only succeed
in making you physically exhausted.

• **HANDLEBARS**
Angle handlebars
towards the slope.

• **BRAKING**
Do not allow the wheels to lock when
braking, or you will risk skidding.

DOWNHILL

To aid stability and balance,
hold your weight well back
and keep the knee on the
inside of the slope pointing
out. When braking, take care
not to lock the wheels.

*Point the knee
on the inside of
the slope, out.*

• **TRACTION**
Aid traction by keeping
your weight well back
over the rear wheel.

• **FEET**
Press down on the pedal that is
away from the slope. This will
keep the bike more upright and
so aid balance and traction.

• **STEERING**
Keep the front wheel turned
slightly into the slope to maximize
traction. Make use of any ruts or
tracks on the slope to aid stability.

GOING DOWN
Riding down **cambers** involves less effort
than going up them, so try not to lose
height unless absolutely necessary.

SKILL

9

DAY 1

ROCKS & DROPS

Definition: *Ways of riding over tough, rocky, and uneven ground*

OFF-ROAD RIDING is all about coping with challenging terrain and all the obstacles it has to offer. To really enjoy mountain biking, you need to reach a level of skill at which you can cope with most of the problems you encounter. There is nothing more dispiriting than being repeatedly defeated by obstacles. The fewer occasions on which you have to dismount, the more fun you will have.

OBJECTIVE: To readily cope with off-road obstacles. *Rating* •••

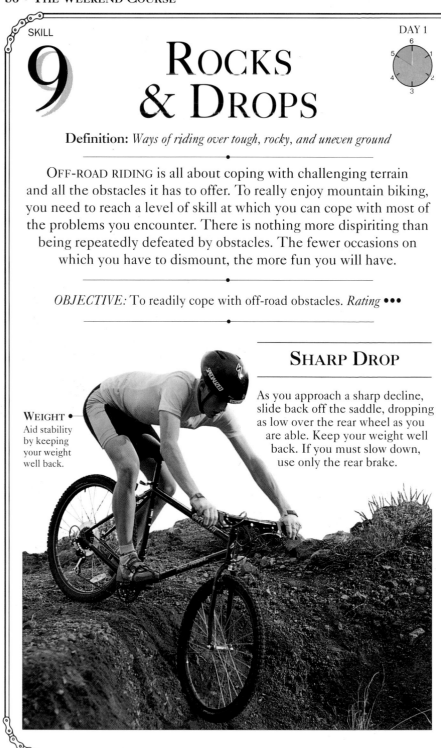

SHARP DROP

WEIGHT •
Aid stability by keeping your weight well back.

As you approach a sharp decline, slide back off the saddle, dropping as low over the rear wheel as you are able. Keep your weight well back. If you must slow down, use only the rear brake.

ROCKY TERRAIN

When you ride over rocky terrain, keep in a low gear so that you can maintain a good, quick pedalling rhythm. Practice will improve your ability to absorb repeated bumps and jolts, rather than letting them knock you out of your rhythm, or even your saddle.

LIFTING THE FRONT WHEEL
Each time you come to a rock, pull up on the handlebars to help the front wheel over it.

KEEP GOING OR GET OFF?

CHOOSING A PATH
The key to riding over rocky terrain is in choosing a path through the obstacles. Plan ahead and anticipate. Speed is of no use here, always ride carefully and slowly.

WHEN TO GIVE UP
Occasionally, the terrain is so tough it is futile to continue cycling. Learn to accept that an all-terrain bike sometimes is not! (See p.50 for details on carrying your bike.)

10 COPING WITH WATER

Definition: *Cycling through water and over waterlogged ground*

THE WATER a mountain biker may encounter ranges from a mere puddle to a waterlogged bog or swamp, and from a shallow stream to a deep and fast-flowing river. Of course, you may prefer to avoid it – and getting soaked – altogether. However, there will be occasions when you will have to choose between cycling through the water or wading through it, carrying your bike over your shoulder. In which case, cycling through is preferable.

OBJECTIVE: To avoid having to wade through water. *Rating* ● ● ●

A CLEAR ROUTE

If you are dealing with clear, shallow water, in which you can see there are no major obstacles, you can simply plough on through. Remember that water impairs the functioning of the brakes, so check them once you are out of the water before proceeding, or you could have a nasty accident.

● **EYES**
Watch out for any sharp or dangerous obstacles as you go through the water, especially if it is deep or murky.

● **BRAKES**
Check the brakes after they get any thorough wetting.

A ROCKY ROUTE

Approach water that has rocks or
boulders in it carefully, and do not
enter it before you have weighed
up the challenge it poses. It is not
worth risking a puncture or a buckled
wheel. Try to pick out a path before
continuing. Cycle through the water
slowly and in a low gear.

PEDALLING IN DEEP WATER
Do not try to rush through water of any
depth. Get in a low gear and keep up a
strong pedalling rhythm.

WATER WISDOM

UNKNOWN WATER
Speeding into unknown water is foolish.
The momentum is hard to maintain and
it is difficult to spot and avoid obstacles.
Also, getting soaked with spray, or even
falling in, is no fun on a cold day.

DEEP GOING
In deep water, currents can throw you off
balance. If full revolutions of the pedals
are difficult, try quarter strokes, beginning
with the pedals vertically aligned and
ending with them horizontal.

11

MUD & SAND SENSE

Definition: *Cycling across loose and unstable surfaces*

SOFT GROUND offers two problems – it is harder for your tyres to gain traction on shifting materials, and your wheels sink into it, increasing the resistance you must overcome to be able to proceed. The key to keeping moving is to go slowly enough to give your tyres the best chance of gaining grip, and also to have the strength and pedalling skill to overcome the rolling resistance such surfaces create. Remember, knobbly tyres can rip into fragile terrain such as bogs and peat. At all costs avoid damaging the environment.

OBJECTIVE: To overcome the twin problems of reduced traction and increased rolling resistance. *Rating* •••

THICK MUD

Proceed through the mud slowly and in your lowest gear, keeping your weight in the saddle to aid traction. If the rear wheel starts to spin, your only option is to dismount and pull the wheel out of the mud.

APPROACH
As you reach mud, drop to your lowest gear and try to progress slowly but steadily. If you speed through, mud will spatter you and the bike.

Damp Sand

Compact sand which has just been revealed by an ebbing tide can provide a smooth, firm surface that offers ideal mountain-biking conditions. But, as sand dries out, it becomes harder for your tyres to grip which causes the rear wheel to both dig into the sand and to slip.

GAINING TRACTION
If your rear wheel spins, drop down the gears and try to go forward with a slow, steady motion.

DEEP MUD & SAND

DEEP MUD
You can cycle through deep mud if it has a firmer surface beneath it for your tyres to bite into. However, you will have to be strong enough to overcome the resistance thick mud creates. The more you practice, the stronger you will get, and the easier skills will become.

DEEP SAND
Deep, dry sand is extremely difficult to cycle over, and so occasionally your only option will be to carry the bike. (See p.50 for details of carrying.)

12 LOG HOPS

Definition: *Shifting weight between wheels*

DAY 2

1 2 3 4 5 6

MUCH OFF-ROAD cycling takes place in woodland and forests, where one of the most frequently encountered obstacles is the fallen tree. Having to get off and lift the bike over each one quickly destroys the pleasure of cycling in such terrain. Once you master the skill of shifting your weight in relation to the bike, you will be able to hop over logs with ease.

OBJECTIVE: To clear obstacles without dismounting. *Rating* •••

TIMING

Timing is crucial so take care in gauging the moment at which you will reach the log. If either of the wheels clip against it you will lose your balance.

• **GEAR**
Select a low gear and approach slowly.

PEDAL •
Have one foot at the start of the pedal stroke.

Step 1
THE APPROACH

Try to approach the log at 90 degrees to avoid the danger of your wheels slipping along its surface. Don't try to cross a log that is broader in section than the distance between the bottom of your chainwheel and the ground. The chainwheel may dig into it, possibly causing severe damage. Begin practising on small logs. As your confidence grows, so will the size of the logs you can hop over.

Step 2
FRONT WHEEL LIFT

As the front wheel touches the log, pull up on the handlebars to bring the wheel onto the top of it. At the same time, shift yourself back in the saddle to minimize the weight on the front wheel.

POSITION
Just before the hop, move back in the saddle.

REAR WHEEL
Get your weight over the rear wheel for a smoother hop.

TRACTION
Compensate for lack of traction by approaching the log hop straight on.

PEDAL
Using the toe clips, yank up your feet to help the lift and hold the bike's weight.

Step 3
FRONT WHEEL OVER

Once the front wheel has cleared the log, completing the first half of the manoeuvre, move your weight over the front of the bike, so that the rear wheel is not loaded down any more than is essential.

WEIGHT
Lean forward to bring your weight over the front wheel.

REAR WHEEL
Weight is shifted off the rear wheel to make lifting easier.

SKILL

12

TOE CLIPS •
Tug up against
your toe clips to
help the lift.

— Step 4 —
REAR WHEEL

When the rear wheel touches
the log, bring your body out
of the saddle, pressing down
on the handlebars. If you are
wearing toe clips, pull up on
them to aid the lift and
help make the log hop
one fluid motion.

• REAR WHEEL
Make sure you have sufficient
forward motion to enable you to
bring the rear wheel onto the log.

• PEDAL
Push down hard on the
lower pedal. This will help
lift the bike over the log.

• FRONT WHEEL
Have as much body
weight as possible
over the front wheel.

— Step 5 —
SAFELY OVER

You know your log hop is successful
once you have managed to lift the
rear wheel up onto the log. The
most common reason for a log hop
to fail is the rear wheel coming to
a dead halt against
the obstacle.

• WEIGHT
Keep your weight
over the front wheel
until the manoeuvre
is completed.

REAR WHEEL
Once the rear wheel
is safely up on the
log, you know your
log hop is a success.

FOOT •
Give a jab on the pedals
to move the bike on.

HOPPING HINTS

BOUNCY TYRES

As you develop in skill and experience you will learn to make the pressure in your tyres work to your advantage. Just before lifting the front wheel, bear down on it. The tyre will spring back, aiding the lift. Likewise with the rear wheel, try a jab down with your feet just before the lift.

TOE CLIPS

A very experienced rider can make hopping over a log look even easier than falling off one, but the technique, like most of the skills, does take practice to perfect. Toe clips make log hopping much easier because they aid you in the hardest part – lifting the rear wheel.

--- Step 6 ---

FOLLOWING THROUGH

Bring the rear wheel down off the log and continue pedalling. Well done! You cleared the log, but that was probably one obstacle among many. The real enjoyment in off-road cycling is being able to clear a whole succession of hazards. So, as soon as you complete one manoeuvre, be prepared to go into the next one.

• HANDS
Be ready for the next obstacle by gripping the handlebars ready for the lift.

BOTTOM •
Shift your weight back into the usual riding position, with your bottom on the saddle to aid rear wheel traction.

FEET •
You should be ready to pedal off straight away.

SKILL

13 BUNNY HOPS

DAY 2

Definition: *Raising both wheels off the ground together*

1   2   3   4   5   6

NOW YOU HAVE REACHED the more intricate skills. Bunny hops can look like the mere indulgences of a stunt rider, but, in fact, they do have practical uses. For example, if you are suddenly faced with an obstacle and cannot change direction or stop before hitting it, jumping over it can be the only alternative to a crash, also, once you can bunny hop, you know that you have extremely highly developed control over your bike. You are demonstrating confidence and ability. However, bunny hops do take practice. Rehearse hopping over a collapsible object, perhaps a cardboard box, until you have perfected your timing.

OBJECTIVE: To clear obstacles without dismounting. *Rating* •••••

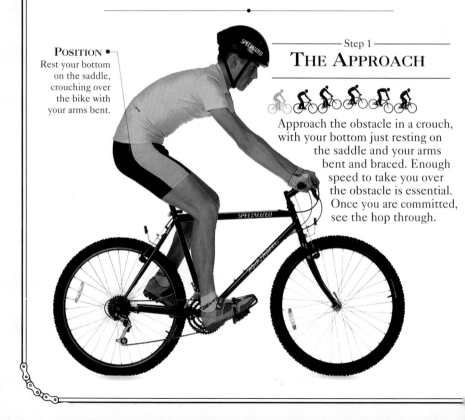

POSITION •
Rest your bottom on the saddle, crouching over the bike with your arms bent.

——— Step 1 ———
THE APPROACH

Approach the obstacle in a crouch, with your bottom just resting on the saddle and your arms bent and braced. Enough speed to take you over the obstacle is essential. Once you are committed, see the hop through.

Step 2

PREPARING TO HOP

Timing is crucial. Lift the bike too soon and you may land on the object; lift too late, and you will crash into it. A split second before the jump, bend the knees and push down hard with hands and feet. This compresses the tyres which will bounce back, giving you an additional lift.

• POSITION
Stand out of the saddle and, just before the jump, push down with hands and feet.

TYRES •
Learn how to use the pressure in your tyres to help the lift.

HIGH HOPS
The higher the lift, the better the hop. To achieve a hop like this, release your weight from the bike, thus allowing it to rise. Keep a firm grip on the bike and it will follow your body up into the air.

Step 3

THE LIFT

Spring up from the bike. As you do so, curl your toes around the pedals and pull up on the handlebars.

✓ REAR WHEEL •
For a stable and controlled hop, keep the rear wheel lower than the front one.

• TOES
Keep your toes curled around the pedals to help gain all the lift you can.

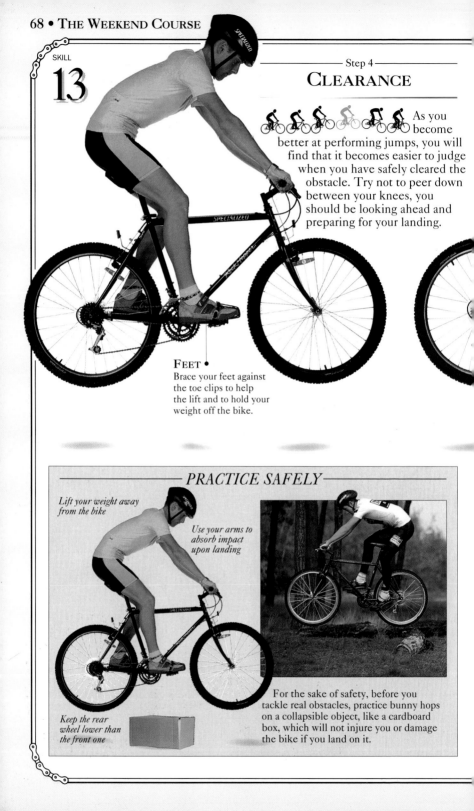

SKILL

13

Step 4

CLEARANCE

As you become better at performing jumps, you will find that it becomes easier to judge when you have safely cleared the obstacle. Try not to peer down between your knees, you should be looking ahead and preparing for your landing.

FEET •
Brace your feet against the toe clips to help the lift and to hold your weight off the bike.

PRACTICE SAFELY

Lift your weight away from the bike

Use your arms to absorb impact upon landing

Keep the rear wheel lower than the front one

For the sake of safety, before you tackle real obstacles, practice bunny hops on a collapsible object, like a cardboard box, which will not injure you or damage the bike if you land on it.

Step 5
THE LANDING

Keep your elbows and knees slightly bent and be ready to use your arms and legs to absorb the impact upon landing. Bring your weight forward over the handlebars and nose the front wheel back to the ground.

• **ARMS**
Brace your arms to absorb the impact as the front wheel comes back to the ground. Make sure you have a firm grip on the handlebars.

• **FRONT WHEEL**
Keep the front wheel pointing straight ahead or you may swerve on landing.

Step 6
RIDING ON

As soon as the front wheel touches the ground, pull your weight back for a stable landing. If you have lost a lot of speed during the hop, you may have to drop a gear or two immediately.

• **POSITION**
Having absorbed the impact of the landing, sit back in the saddle.

GEARS •
Be prepared to move down the gears quickly if you have drastically slowed down.

DAY 2

14 FRONT WHEEL PIVOTS

Definition: *Sharp turns with only the front wheel on the ground*

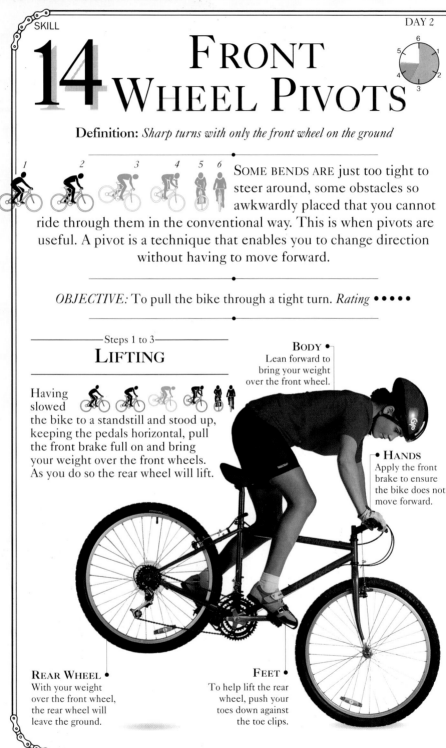

SOME BENDS ARE just too tight to steer around, some obstacles so awkwardly placed that you cannot ride through them in the conventional way. This is when pivots are useful. A pivot is a technique that enables you to change direction without having to move forward.

OBJECTIVE: To pull the bike through a tight turn. *Rating* •••••

―――――Steps 1 to 3―――――
LIFTING

Having slowed the bike to a standstill and stood up, keeping the pedals horizontal, pull the front brake full on and bring your weight over the front wheels. As you do so the rear wheel will lift.

BODY •
Lean forward to bring your weight over the front wheel.

• **HANDS**
Apply the front brake to ensure the bike does not move forward.

REAR WHEEL •
With your weight over the front wheel, the rear wheel will leave the ground.

FEET •
To help lift the rear wheel, push your toes down against the toe clips.

WEIGHT •
Keep your weight
well forward.

PIVOTING

Once the rear wheel is off the
ground, you can shift it to the
left or right, by moving your
body in the required direction
before bringing the wheel back
to the ground.

• **HANDLEBARS**
It may help to twist
the handlebars in the
opposite direction to
that of the rear wheel.

FEET •
Keep your feet in
the horizontal position.

LANDING

Make up
for any
inaccuracy in the pivot by ensuring
you are steering in the appropriate
direction to continue when the front
wheel lands. To move off smoothly,
it is essential to time correctly the
landing of the rear wheel, releasing
the brake, and pushing the pedals.

• **WEIGHT**
Move your weight
back as you land.

• **BRAKE**
Do not release the
brake too soon.

MORE THAN ONE PIVOT
With practice it is possible to move the bike
through angles of as much as 180 degrees
using a series of pivots. To do so, repeat the
process described above two or more times.

PIVOT PRACTICE
Practice the pivot on flat,
grassy areas or similar, where
there are none of the distractions
that a ride through rough and
varied terrain can bring.

SKILL

DAY 2

15 REAR WHEEL PIVOTS

Definition: *Tight turns with only the rear wheel on the ground*

THE REAR WHEEL PIVOT is useful when you come right up against an insurmountable obstacle. It enables you to pull the front of the bike into the air and land it where the way ahead is clear. It is much more efficient than the alternative of putting your feet down and dragging the bike around.

OBJECTIVE: To avoid an obstacle without dismounting. *Rating* • • • • •

•**HANDS**
Pull up on
the handlebars.

─────── Steps 1 to 3 ───────
LIFTING

Once you
have stopped pedalling
and are standing up on
the pedals, apply the rear
brake. Shift your weight
well back and pull up on
the handlebars. Aid the
manoeuvre by lifting
up against the toe clips.

BE PREPARED
The secret to a successful
pivot is being prepared.
As soon as you spot an
impassable obstacle, stop
pedalling, stand up on the
pedals, and once you reach
the obstacle, apply the rear
brake. Now start the pivot.

• **FRONT WHEEL**
With the front wheel off
the ground, the bike can
swing round without any
forward motion.

LEGS •
Bend, then straighten,
the legs as you lift
the front of the
bike to assist in
the manoeuvre.

HANDS •
Pull on the
handlebars
to help the
bike pivot
right or
left.

Step 4
PIVOTING

 Use your
body to
pivot the bike, either right or left as
required, by moving your weight in
the desired direction. Only a gentle
motion is needed when the wheel
is off the ground.

• FRONT WHEEL
Swing the front wheel
away from the obstacle
blocking your path.

• FEET
Keep your feet in a
horizontal position.
Do not bear down
during the manoeuvre.

• HANDS
Release the rear
brake as the front
wheel lands.

• FEET
Be prepared to start
pedalling as soon as
the pivot is over.

Steps 5 & 6
LANDING

It takes
skill to
land the bike in the exact path you
need to follow to proceed unhindered.
As with front wheel pivots, you can
help compensate for any inaccuracy in
the pivot by ensuring you are steering
in the correct direction to continue
once the front wheel lands.

CONFIDENCE

Confidence in your own abilities means
you are likely to master many, if not all
of the skills in this book fairly quickly.
However, if you find the thought of a
pivot daunting, do not attempt it until
you have gained more confidence on
your bike. Then, break the skill down
to its component parts, as shown on this
page. Understand each element, then
put them back together to do the pivot.

FRONT WHEEL •
Have your weight back in
the normal cycling position
when the front wheel lands.

PEDALLING •
Once safely out of
the pivot, straighten
the handlebars and
start pedalling.

SKILL

DAY 2

16 SAFE FALLING

Definition: *Parting company with your bike*

MUCH OF THIS BOOK has been about how to perform all sorts of manoeuvres on a bike, without having an accident. However, if you do fall off, there are techniques for minimizing the risk of injury. Even if you decide not to practice this skill, bear the following advice in mind and follow it should you find yourself being thrown off the bike or tumbling over the handlebars.

OBJECTIVE: Avoiding injury in an accident. *Rating* •••••

FALLING

If you take a fall, you will realize just how important safety clothing is, particularly knee and elbow pads which are advisable for when riding over rough and rocky ground. Do not extend your arms to try and save yourself, you are more likely to break a limb. Instead, try to turn a fall into a roll so that you land on your back and slow down gently.

ARMS •
Do not extend your arms to break a fall.

HEAD •
Keep your head tucked under as you land. This is where your crash helmet comes into its own.

OVER THE HANDLEBARS
A fall over the handlebars is one of the most common cycling accidents. If you wear a crash helmet, and turn your fall into a roll, you should be able to avoid serious injury.

FALL RECOVERY

After a fall, follow these guidelines.
- Catch your breath before standing up.
- Check yourself for injuries.
- Examine the bike too. Check the front wheel for buckles. See if the forks are bent out of line, or if the handlebars are twisted.
- If the fall has been quite a shock, rest for a while and drink some water.
- If you came off because the terrain was too tough, carry or push the bike until the going gets easier
- If your helmet has taken a knock, replace it before going on your next ride. Once they have absorbed an impact, helmets cease to function at their optimum.

LANDING

One of the most painful cycling accidents can be landing on top of your bike. With a bit of luck you will have more velocity than the machine and will land beyond it. Sometimes, there may be nothing you can do to avoid falling onto the bike but you can at least be aware of the danger and attempt, when the bike goes one way, to launch yourself in another direction. On landing, try to roll so that the impact is minimized and you slow down relatively gently.

A TEXTBOOK LANDING
This is a perfect landing. It looks more like gymnastics than an accident, and, of course, the soft bed of sand to fall on helps.

• POSTURE
If you can land on your shoulders you will avoid any danger of a head injury. Coming down flat on your back could damage the spine, so a curved posture and a gentle roll is ideal.

• BACK
If you end up back on your feet, fine, but don't be afraid to stay down and get your breath back.

AFTER THE WEEKEND

Now you have mastered the basics you can be more adventurous

YOUR LEARNING WEEKEND has given you a firm grounding in mountain biking technique. If you coped with it reasonably well, you can rest assured that you know enough about mountain biking skills to hold your head up in any company. The wonderful world of mountain biking is now open to you. You can venture into the toughest terrain without being a danger to yourself or others, you can turn up at race meetings and take part as a novice, you could even make the first tentative plans for an expedition. However, before you set off for the Sahara or Everest, you need to gain a lot more experience. The next stage in testing your mettle could perhaps be a fortnight in one of the world's more challenging mountain bike terrains. As you progress, remember one thing – there is no point pushing yourself too hard, trying to perform outside the limits of your abilities, and coming to grief. Take things as slowly as you need to. And good luck!

GAINING EXPERIENCE

Becoming a competent, all-round mountain biker

THERE ARE LIKELY to be areas of this course in which you excelled, and others in which you did less well. To become a good, all-round off-roader, you need to concentrate on your weaknesses. Take a look back through the sixteen skills you have tried to master and give yourself marks out of ten for each. A nine or ten is excellent and no further practice is necessary. A six to eight means a little more practice is required and a five, or less, means further sustained effort is needed. It may be that you find some skills are simply too technical for you. If so, concentrate on just the basic skills and straightforward, off-road cycling where the more advanced skills like front and rear wheel pivots will not be needed. Once you have mastered the basics, then you can gradually start practising the more difficult skills again.

A ROCKY PATH
On loose, bumpy ground, speed is not of the essence. Get in a low gear, move slowly but surely, and keep your pedalling rate up to 90 revolutions per minute (p.57).

AVOIDING OBSTACLES

Spotting obstacles and avoiding them may sound routine but it is a key skill, and is far more important than riding fast (p.58).

DEEP WATER

Deep water throws up several problems. If you cannot see the bottom, you are hard pressed to judge whether you can cope with the depth, or to steer a course through its obstacles. One thing that holds many people back is the simple fear of getting wet. In cold weather it is to be avoided, but if it is a warm, sunny day, it can actually be fun (p.59).

LOG HOPS

Lifting the bike in a log or bunny hop proves very difficult for some. If you are learning in a group, those who are good at a particular skill can give valuable advice to those who are struggling. Often, a friend can see where you are going wrong when you cannot, and can help correct a fault quickly (pp.62-69).

UPHILL RIDING

A steep hill is a test of stamina, balance, and judgement. The more you practice, the steeper the inclines that you will be able to cope with. It is far better to be able to stay on the bike going up a hill. Having to get off, push, or carry the bike breaks up the day's cycling and can be demoralizing (pp.46-47).

STUNTS

Learning the exciting and elaborate tricks of mountain biking

STUNT RIDING MAY SEEM like the frivolous side of mountain biking, or even the dangerous antics of an immature racer. If you hold this view then stunts are probably not for you. There is, however, another side to this sort of flamboyant cycling. For a rider to be able to cycle along backwards, on one wheel, in a series of hops, or even with the front wheel removed, takes more than sheer bravado. It takes a consummate mastery of the bike. There is no better display of a mountain biker's level of ability than seeing him or her perform the sort of stunts that appear on this page. Seeing a bike put through its paces by a top stunt rider is as exhilarating and exciting as watching a brilliant downhill skier or a top-flight gymnast. So why not try it, you may like it!

THE WHEELIE

Start with the front wheel off the ground and the right pedal just below the horizontal. Press your right foot onto the right pedal, bring the other foot onto the left pedal and start pedalling.

WHEELIE PRACTICE
Wheelies work well on firm ground, but while learning, it is wise to practice on soft ground only. The secret to a successful wheelie is plenty of practice and learning how to balance the bike.

TOE CLIPS
Either abandon toe clips or keep them loose. If you topple backwards, you need to be able to free your feet quickly.

LAUNCH OFF

As with a conventional wheelie, you can also launch yourself into this stunt with the front of the bike raised up off the ground.

LOOK NO WHEEL!

Real experts can wheelie without having the front wheel on the bike. Taking the wheel off makes the front of the bike much lighter, and also makes the stunt look particularly impressive. Do not attempt this stunt yourself until you are a skilled wheelie rider, and always perform on soft earth, or you risk wrecking your forks.

• LIFTING THE FORKS

With the forks resting on the ground and the right pedal just past the vertical, yank up on the handlebars and start to pedal very hard. The front of the bike will lift.

——TABLE TOPPING——

Table topping is one stage on from bunny hopping. It is used by those who compete in high jump events and the experts can manage around 1m (3ft) in height. The technique is to bend the legs, lifting the bike, and then angle it either to the left or right to give added clearance. This also makes the stunt look even more impressive.

BALANCE

Beware: without the front wheel the bike will handle very differently.

EXPERIENCED ONLY

Table topping is one of the toughest stunts to perform. Therefore, like the other feats on this page, it should only be attempted on soft ground by adept and experienced mountain bikers.

TOE CLIPS •

If wearing toe clips, keep them loose so that you can bale off the back of the bike quickly and easily.

JOINING A CYCLE CLUB

What a cycle club has to offer and how to join one

•

TO PROGRESS IN ANY SPORT it is a good idea to get in touch with
people who share your interest in it. The benefits are twofold: if a
sport involves a social element it is more appealing; and to practice
it with others gives you a measure of your own proficiency, and a
gauge of how you are progressing. There are those who enjoy the
solitude of off-road cycling in remote areas, but most people find
such adventures far more enjoyable when they are shared with
others. After all, what is the point of scaling a mountain on two
wheels if you have no one to share in the achievement and to brag
about it with afterwards? Cycle clubs cater for all, from the novice to
the expert, the one thing in common being their love of the sport.

A CLUB FOR ALL

There are many local cycle clubs, some made up
of dedicated, madcap racers, others for those who
enjoy a pleasant leisurely ride over gentle grassland
with plenty of opportunity for liquid refreshment.

FINDING A CLUB

One of the best ways to learn about clubs is by reading the notice boards or by talking to the staff in your local bike shop. Both can be valuable information sources about biking events. The many mountain bike publications now available are also a good source of the latest news.

ORGANIZED OUTINGS
Cycle clubs will organize outings. These may vary from a leisurely, Sunday afternoon ride to a real endurance test.

SERIOUS FUN!
You may be into serious riding, or simply into eccentric ideas like this mountain bike tandem. Whichever you choose, mountain biking is always fun.

WELCOME TO CLUB LAND

Today, most towns and cities have a club and, almost invariably, you will be welcomed with open arms, whatever your level of proficiency. These cycle clubs organize everything to do with mountain biking, from races and stunt competitions to holidays.

RACE THE WORLD
One of the wonderful aspects of mountain biking is the opportunity to travel. This is especially true if you want to participate in the many races that are held throughout the world. Most countries now have a cycling organization that can help you with the necessary arrangements.

COMPETING

Mountain bike competitions & how to enter

ONE OF THE APPEALS of mountain biking competitively is that you can slip into it so easily. Most mountain bike races have a section for novices in which you can race round the same track as the big stars but pit yourself against other beginners. Small scale races may be organized by a club, a cycle shop, a council, or other community group. More formal events will be sanctioned and overseen by a professional body.

MASS START
Everyone starts the race together, novices with experts.

START

Pits

The edge

Hero's tumble

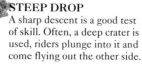

Two tier climb

Chickens' route

STEEP DROP
A sharp descent is a good test of skill. Often, a deep crater is used, riders plunge into it and come flying out the other side.

Canal bottom

END STRETCH
The hazards behind you, speed is now of the essence.

FINISH STRAIGHT

Lap lane

Top end

Martin wood

Log jump

Rover alley

Pits

MOUND
A tough surface like this takes dexterity and co-ordination. This is where the experts are distinguished from the novices.

DOWNHILL
Going downhill is where a rider can win or lose a race. Some riders are fearful of coming off the bike, while others are braver and use the descents to leave everyone else behind.

TOURING

Setting off for freedom, excitement and adventure

MOUNTAIN BIKING GIVES you a great sense of freedom, but touring, when you travel for several days, weeks, even months without returning to base, can make you feel truly independent and adventurous. The drawback of such travels is that you will have to carry most of what you need – perhaps absolutely everything that you need – with you on the journey. A bike loaded down with gear will not be a great bunny hop machine, but the loss of performance can be made up for by the heightened sense of adventure.

CARRYING

Apart from a backpack, you can fit **panniers** to your bike. There is now a wide range of these carriers available, attaching to the rear of the bike, the handlebars, and sitting alongside the front wheel.

CONQUERORS
Above: Two of the world's foremost mountain bike adventurers are Richard and Nick Crane. They have conquered deserts and mountains.

PANNIERS
Pack these **panniers** with equal weight or steering suffers.

TRANSPORTING YOUR BIKE
Transporting your bike is easy with a car rack, but ensure it doesn't cover the car's number plate, as it is illegal.

A BIKER'S TENT

A car can transport your bike and tent to your starting point, but from then on you will have to carry your home on your bike. Therefore, go for a tent that is very light and compact. The one below actually uses the bike as a support.

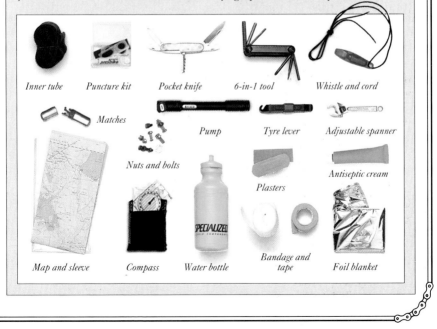

ESSENTIAL EQUIPMENT

When touring, aim to be self-sufficient. If you are to avoid time consuming detours to get supplies or help, try to take all that you will need with you. At the very least you should take the essential tools and first aid kit. (See pp.32-33.) Always wear a distress whistle on a lanyard around your neck. It could prove vital in signalling for help should you find yourself all alone, lying injured in a remote place.

Inner tube   Puncture kit   Pocket knife   6-in-1 tool   Whistle and cord

Matches   Pump   Tyre lever   Adjustable spanner

Nuts and bolts   Antiseptic cream

Plasters

Map and sleeve   Compass   Water bottle   Bandage and tape   Foil blanket

ULTIMATE ADVENTURES

Some of the most exciting and magical places to mountain bike

MOUNTAIN BIKES HAVE BEEN taken to the far corners of the earth, to the top of Mount Kilimanjaro, across the Sahara, and through rainforests. They have been ridden down mines and potholes and people have even parachuted sitting astride them. If you could go anywhere in the world in search of the most thrilling mountain biking experience, where would you go? The following is my personal list of ultimate adventures, some are incredibly tough, all are magical.

THE GOBI DESERT

Right: The cousins Richard and Nick Crane conquered the Gobi Desert on bikes that were half mountain bike, half Tour de France racers. They were heading for the point in the world farthest from any ocean. They identified this point in the Gobi Desert. Nick Crane described the Gobi as "a shallow bowl of small, dead, desert shrubs set in a million acres of sand".

KILIMANJARO

Below: Kilimanjaro, at 5,895m (19,340ft), is the highest mountain in Africa. Nick Crane, who has ridden it, says the first 4,725m (15,500ft) are relatively easy riding, before you hit the snow and ice, and that the summit is incredible. In his own words: "Riding around the lip of the volcano crater is like balancing on the edge of a giant teacup, and coming down is the freewheel of a lifetime ".

PARAPENTE
Is there anything madder than parachuting on a mountain bike? Probably not, but fans of the sport rave about the thrill of it all, and the skill needed to be able to land and pedal off before the parachute envelopes you.

THE ST.ELIAS MOUNTAINS
The 500km (310 mile) long mountain range of St.Elias is shredded by glaciers and split by canyons. Almost completely bereft of trails, it had never been crossed on wheels until defeated by mountain bikers in 1988.

MOUNT KOSCIUSKO
In skiing regions worldwide, from the Alps in Europe to Whistler in Canada, mountain biking has established itself as the ideal sport for seasons when skiing isn't possible. Many mountain bikers came to the sport from skiing, as a way of enjoying the mountains all the year round. Australia's Blue Mountains, Snowy Mountains, and Mount Kosciusko, provide ideal mountain biking country. The Blue Mountains in particular attract many bikers.

DURANGO

The Colorado trail is 750km (466 miles) long and runs from Denver. The world mountain biking championships were held here in 1990.

BIG BEND PARK

The Chihuahuan Desert in a forgotten corner of Texas, down on the Mexican border, is an area of arid plains and mountains. This is real wilderness, and harsh cycling terrain. NASA rehearsed the Apollo moon landings here, and it is the setting for the opening sequences for Wim Wender's movie *Paris, Texas*.

THE RIDGEWAY

This green road, stretching from the Thames to Avebury is gentle chalk downland, and is probably the oldest road in Europe. It has never been tarmacked or modernized in any way, but is still open to all vehicles.

PICOS MOUNTAIN

Perfect for snow-biking, if you are brave or foolhardy enough. The Picos rise to 1,524m (5,000ft) and run for 32km (20 miles) behind Santander, on Spain's northern coast. They are ideal for really exhilarating descents.

GLOSSARY

Words in *italic* are glossary entries.

A

• **Adjusting barrel** The nut that can be turned by hand, enabling you to adjust the tension on the brake and the *derailleur* cables.
• **Adjusting screw** The screw that can be used to adjust both the front and rear *derailleurs*.
• **Allen keys** This is an hexagonal tool for adjusting Allen bolts, which are often used for fixing gearing, braking, and other mechanisms on mountain bikes.

B

• **Brake cable housing** The outer casing and protector of the brake and gear cables.
• **Bottom bracket** The bracket found at the point at which *seat tube* and *down tube* join. The bottom bracket houses the *crank* shaft.

C

• **Cable clamp** The point at which a brake or *derailleur* cable is held tight against the brake or derailleur.
• **Cable clamp bolt** The nut and bolt that hold the *cable clamp* tight against a cable.
• **Cable stop** The metal caps, also known as ferrals, fitted onto the end of the outer casing of the brake cables.
• **Camber** Any kind of a slope. They are usually ridden at an angle.
• **Cantilever brake** This is a brake mechanism comprising two separate arms. One arm is fixed on either side of the wheel.
• **Chainset** The three sprockets or cogs, also known as chainrings, that are attached to the *crank* shaft.
• **Chain stays** The tubes that make up part of the bicycle frame. They run horizontally out from the *bottom bracket* on either side of the rear wheel.
• **Crank** Lever arm that joins a pedal to the chainwheel and *bottom bracket*.

D

• **Dead spot** The points at the bottom and top of each stroke during the pedalling cycle, when neither leg is in the powerful part of its pedal stroke.
• **Derailleur** A mechanism through which a bicycle chain runs. It can move the chain between a number of cogs.
• **Derailleur cage** The lower half of the front end of the rear *derailleur*.
• **Down tube** The lower tube in a bicycle frame, running between the head tube and the *bottom bracket*.
• **Drop outs** The slots found in the forks and in the bicycle's frame into which the front and rear axles slot and are tightened against.
• **Dust caps** The protective coverings on an inner tube valve. They are also found on the *cranks* to prevent their bolts from rusting.

F

• **Flange** The rings that lace the spokes into the hub and rim of a wheel. There are two flanges to each hub.
• **Freewheel** The cluster of rear cogs or sprockets attached to the rear wheel which are an essential part of the gearing mechanism. They continue to rotate even when you have ceased pedalling, thereby slowing the bike down and bringing it to a gentle stop.

Coping with a steep drop

M

• **Mounting pivot bolt** This is the bolt that holds the rear *derailleur* or the mechanism onto the bicycle's frame. The rear derailleur or mechanism pivots on the *mounting bolt* whenever the gear is being changed.

N

• **Nipple** Nipples join the individual spokes to the rim of the wheel. They can be loosened or tightened to straighten a slightly bent or buckled wheel. This can be done using your hands or a spoke key.

P

• **Panniers** Large bags that can be attached to a bicycle. They are usually placed one on either side of the wheel so that the bike is weighted evenly.

S

• **Seat cluster** Point at which the *seat stays*, *seat tube*, and, sometimes, the *top tube* are joined.
• **Seat post** The tube beneath the saddle that slots into the *seat tube*.
• **Seat post release** The quick-release bolt found at the top of the *seat tube* that allows instant adjustment of the saddle height.
• **Seat stays** These are the higher tubes attached to the bicycle frame on which the rear brake is mounted.
• **Seat tube** The tube that runs from the *top tube* to the *bottom bracket* into which the *seat post* slots.
• **Spoke** The length of wire running from the hub of the wheel to the rim. It can be adjusted using the *nipple* to straighten the wheel.
• **Straddle cable** The cable that links the two halves of a caliper brake.

T

• **Top tube** The top horizontal bar on a frame, also known as the cross bar.
• **Travel limit adjuster bolt** Bolt used to adjust the position of the *derailleur* by preventing the chain from going over the top cog or off the bottom cog.
• **Tubular tyres** These are hard tyres that have no inner tube, but are glued to the wheel's rim instead. They are mainly used for fast road riding.

TOP TEN

Key rules of competitive mountain biking:

1. Marshalls will cast a blind eye to riders rolling forward slightly before the gun sounds, but they will not take lightly to a false start.
2. Once the race has begun, a rider is not permitted to change any part of their bike. Repairs may be made, but only with the equipment and tools the rider is carrying with him.
3. If the rider takes any equipment or help from someone not in the race, he can be disqualified.
4. There is an exception to the above rule. Another rider in the race can give their tools or inner tube to a fellow competitor, if they so wish.
5. Food and water can be handed to riders whenever it is needed. However, some events only permit refreshments in designated areas.
6. In a cross country race, the riders must ride the designated course set or face the risk of disqualification.
7. If there happens to be a rider you are coming up to lap or overtake, give a good clear warning that you want to come through and on what side.
8. If you come across walkers or horse riders on the course (they may not know about the race) be polite, and slow down if you need to.
9. Race within your limits and try to be considerate to other riders.
10. The main rule not to forget in mountain bike racing, is to have fun!

Tackling a steep ascent

INDEX

GETTING IN TOUCH

The British Cycling Federation,
36, Rockingham Road,
Kettering,
Northants NN16 8GH
Tel: 01536 412211

Welsh Mountain Bike Club,
52, Beach Road,
Porthcawl
Mid-Glamorgan SF36 5NH
Tel: 01656 712922

ACKNOWLEDGMENTS

Andy Bull and Dorling Kindersley would like to thank the following
for their valuable help and expertise in the production of this book:

David Hemming for modelling and being a valuable consultant.
Gail Hayward, and Tom Shone for modelling. Philip Gatward and his
team: Jeremy Hopley and Toby MacFarlone-Pond (photography assistants),
and Richard Blakey (set and prop builder), not forgetting the local pizza
shop who helped us through the many long, late, but always fun, photo
shoots. Jenny Jordan and Dawn Lane (make-up artists). Debbie DeMeritte
from Evans Cycles (1 The Cut, Waterloo) for the generous and trusting
loaning of their cyclewear, equipment, and touring bike. *SPECIALIZED*
(SBC (UK) LTD) for the mountain bikes, and Been Bag for cycle gear.
Sarah Larter for editorial assistance and Hilary Bird for the index.
Rob Shone and Janos Marffy for line drawings, John Woodcock
for colour illustrations (pp.84-85).

The following for the use of photographs: StockFile; Dave Roman
(p.26*tr*), Steven Behr (p.27, p.90*tr*, p.91*tr* &*bl*),
Robert Newhouse (p.90*tr*), Jill Daun (p.90*b*), Peter Blake (p.91*tl*),
John Hairsine (p.91*br*). Nick Crane (p.86*mr* & pp.89-90).
t: top, *b:* bottom, *m:* middle, *r:* right, *l:* left.